National Curric

English

Practice Book for

Year 3

SCHOLASTIC

Book End, Range Road, Witney, Oxfordshire, OX29 0YD
www.scholastic.co.uk
© 2014, Scholastic Ltd
6789 6789012345

British Library Cataloguing-in-Publication Data
A catalogue record for this book is available from the British Library.

ISBN 978-1407-12896-2
Printed by Bell & Bain Ltd, Glasgow

Editorial
Rachel Morgan, Melissa Somers, Sarah Sodhi, Catherine Baker
and Fiona Tomlinson

Design
Scholastic Design Team: Neil Salt, Nicolle Thomas
and Oxford Designers & Illustrators Ltd

Cover Design
Neil Salt

Illustration
Aleksander Sotirovski (Beehive Illustration)

Acknowledgements
The publishers gratefully acknowledge permission to reproduce the following
copyright material: **David Higham Associates** for the use of a text
extract from *Midnight for Charlie Bone* by Jenny Nimmo. Text © 2002, Jenny
Nimmo (2002, Egmont). **Kingfisher Publications plc** for the use of two
extracts from *First Facts: Science* by Barbara Reseigh. Text © 1994, Kingfisher
Publications plc (1994, Kingfisher Publications plc). **Peters, Fraser and
Dunlop** for the use of 'I'm just going out for a moment' from *Wouldn't You
Like To Know* by Michael Rosen. Poem © 1977, Michael Rosen (1977, Andre
Deutsch). **Paul Cookson** for the use of 'Every game's a home game with
my footy family' from Inter Gillbrook. Poem © 2006, Paul Cookson (2006,
The Way Ahead). **Walker Books Ltd** for the use of an extract from *The
Mousehole Cat* by Antonia Barber, illustrated by Nicola Bayley. Text © 1990,
Antonia Barber (1990, Walker Books Ltd) and for the use of an extract 'Hot
Sleepysaurus' from *Our Sleepysaurus* by Martin Waddell, illustrated by Clive
Scruton. Text © 1988, Martin Waddell (1988, Walker Books).

Every effort has been made to trace copyright holders for the works reproduced
in this book, and the publishers apologise for any inadvertent omissions.

Contents

Why buy this book?

The 100 Lessons series has been designed to support the introduction of the new National Curriculum in schools in England. The new curriculum is more challenging in English and includes the requirement for children's understanding to be secure before moving on. These practice books will help your child practise all of the skills they will learn at school, including some topics they might not have encountered previously.

How to use this book?

- The content is divided into National Curriculum topics (for example, Spelling, Grammar, Comprehension and so on). Find out what your child is doing in school and dip into the relative practice activities as required.

- Let your child know you are sharing the activities and support if necessary using the helpful quick tips at the top of most pages.

- Keep the working time short and come back to an activity if your child finds it too difficult. Ask your child to note any areas of difficulty. Don't worry if your child does not 'get' a concept first time, as children learn at different rates and content is likely to be covered throughout the school year.

- Check your child's answers using the answers section on www.scholastic.co.uk/100practice/englishy3

- You will also find additional interactive activities for your child to play on the website.

- Give lots of encouragement and tick off the progress chart as your child completes each chapter.

How to use the book?

This tells you which topic you're working on.

This is the title of the activity.

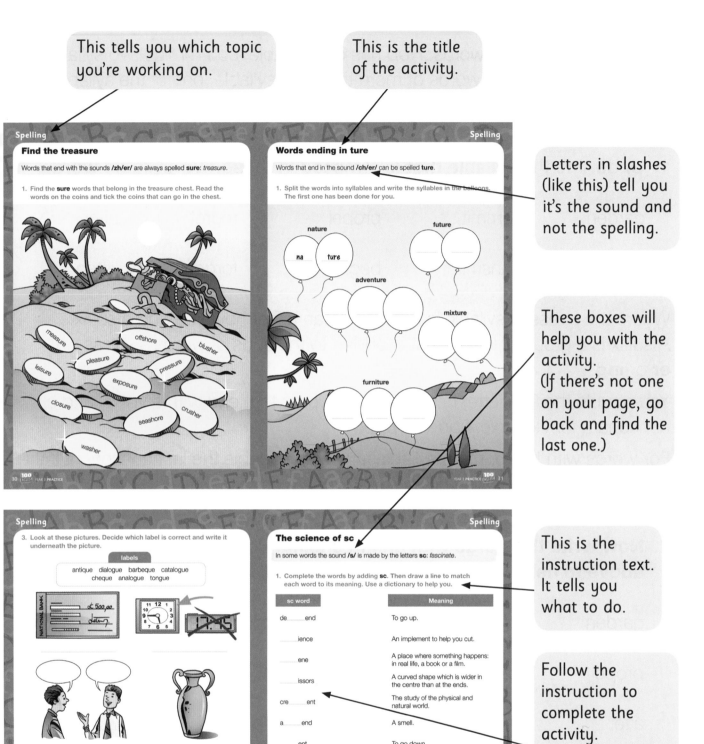

Letters in slashes (like this) tell you it's the sound and not the spelling.

These boxes will help you with the activity.
(If there's not one on your page, go back and find the last one.)

This is the instruction text. It tells you what to do.

Follow the instruction to complete the activity.

You might have to write on lines, in boxes, draw or circle things.

If you need help, ask an adult!

To double or not!

Syllables are parts of words. *Hop* has one syllable, *control* has two syllables: *con/trol*. When we say words of more than one syllable, one of the syllables is said slightly louder than the others – it is **stressed**.

1. **Underline the syllable that is stressed in these two-syllable words.**

garden	commit	propel	regret	alter
wonder	transmit	begin	forget	listen

Where the stressed syllable is in a word, can affect how you add a suffix. A suffix is a group of letters that is added to the ends of words such as **ed**, **er** or **ing**.

You double the final letter in one-syllable words that end with a vowel and a consonant for example, *hop – hopped*.

For words with two or more syllables, you only double the last consonant if the stressed syllable is at the end: *con**trol** – controlled* but **vi**sit – visiting*.

2. **Now write the words with an ing ending. Look back at the rules above to help you decide whether to double the consonant.**

garden _____   commit _____

propel _____   regret _____

alter _____   wonder _____

transmit _____   begin _____

forget _____   listen _____

Adding 'ing'

You add **ing** to verbs to show the action is happening now: *I am walking* or to words that describe something people do: *I love painting; I enjoy sailing*. Many words add the suffix **ing** without any change of spelling: *shout – shouting*. Words ending in **e** drop the **e** before adding **ing**: *giggle – giggling*.

Remember that sometimes you double the final consonant – see page 6 to remind yourself.

1. Add the suffix **ing** to the verbs below. The first one has been done for you.

Word	Word + ing
clap	*clapping*
go	
hope	
submit	
pull	
ride	
prefer	
permit	
walk	
patrol	

Adding ed

You add **ed** to words to show the past tense. Try to remember these rules:
Many words add **ed** without any change of spelling: *jump – jumped*.
Words ending in **e**, drop the **e** before adding **ed**: *hope – hoped*.

Remember that sometimes you double the final consonant – see page 6 to remind yourself.

1. **Help the ed machine. Add ed to the verbs below. The first one has been done for you.**

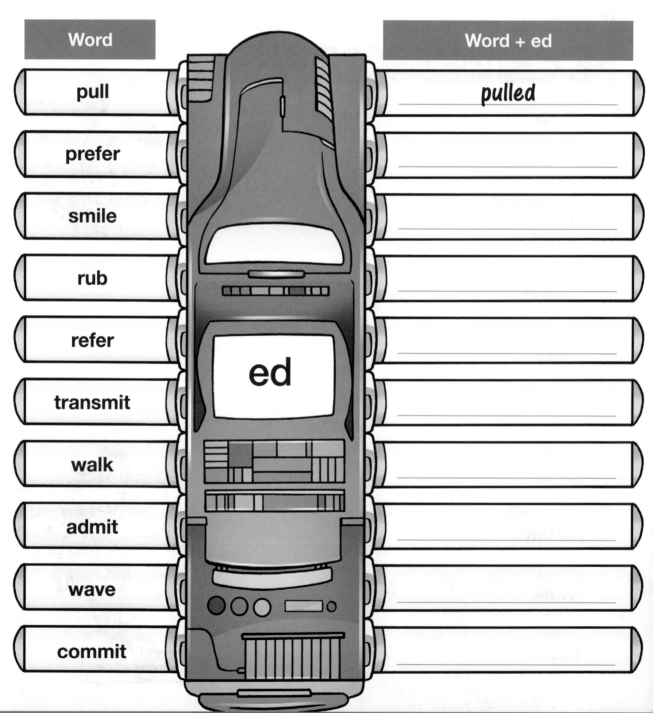

Word	Word + ed
pull	pulled
prefer	
smile	
rub	
refer	
transmit	
walk	
admit	
wave	
commit	

Adding er

When adding **er** to verbs you can create a noun.
Many verbs add **er** without any change of spelling: *teach – teacher*.
Words ending in **e**, drop the **e** before adding **er**: *bake – baker*.

Remember that sometimes you double the final consonant – see page 6 to remind yourself.

1. **Karen is knitting er jumpers. Add er to the verbs below and write them on the jumpers. The first one has been done for you.**

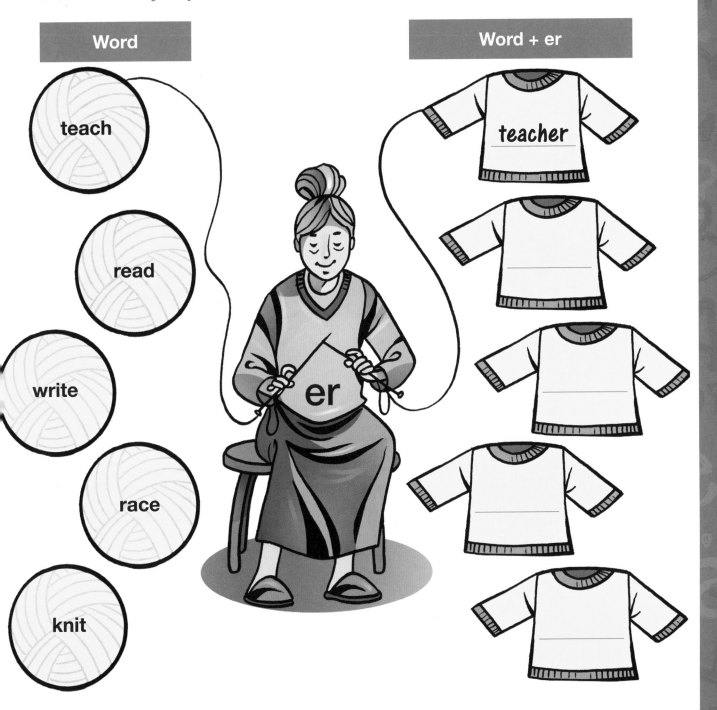

Word	Word + er
teach	teacher
read	
write	
race	
knit	

When i becomes a spy and disguises as a y!

In some words the long vowel **/igh/** sound is spelled with a **y**: *spy*, *by*, *my*. But in some words with a short vowel **/i/** sound, the **/i/** can also be spelled with a **y**: *gym*.

There are no rules to when you use a **y** or not – they just have to be learned!

1. **The words below are not spelled correctly. Correct them by changing the i to a y.**

gim　　　　　_____

Egipt　　　　_____

mistery　　　_____

sillable　　　_____

mith　　　　_____

simbol　　　_____

cristal　　　_____

simptom　　_____

2. **Can you solve this mystery? These words each have a missing letter. Add the missing letter and then draw a line to match each one to its meaning.**

A religious song sung mainly in churches.

P____ramid

A shape with four triangular sides and one square bottom.

Pterodact____l

Something that we breathe.

H____mn

A dinosaur that flies.

S____rup

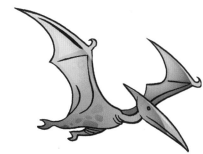

A thick liquid that is often sweet.

Ox____gen

Can you shout trouble?

The letters **ou** can make three sounds: **/oo/** – *you*, **/ow/** – *shout* and **/u/** – *trouble*.

There are no rules about when to use the different sounds – you just have to know them! But there are fewer words with the **ou** spelling for the short vowel **/u/** sound.

1. **Read the words below and circle the ones which have the sound /u/ as in *trouble*.**

double

touch

round

you

cousin

young

loud

about

youth

country

soup

house

route

2. Read the story below. Circle the spelling mistakes and correct them underneath.

The yung child got himself into truble because he hit his cusin. He didn't

_____

like the cusin tuching his toys and he wanted to stop him. The cusin was

_____

not very nice and he encuraged the yung child to tuch the expensive vase.

_____

The vase broke and the yung child was told off. The yung child said it was

_____

the cusin who had persuaded him to tuch the vase. Then the cusin stuck

_____

out his tongue and made the yung child cry.

_____

Change the meaning of a word

Prefixes are a group of letters put in front of words that often change the meanings of words.

dis means *not* or *opposite of*, as in *disagree*

mis means *not* or *wrong*, as in *misunderstand*

1. Change the meanings of these words by adding **dis** or **mis** to the beginning. Match the words to the prefix and then write the new words in the spaces.

Word	Prefix	New word
like		
match		
obey	**mis**	
lead		
place		
fit		
honest		
fortune	**dis**	
direct		
appear		

2. These sentences do not make sense. Rewrite them by adding the correct prefix, dis or mis.

I like bad smells as they make me sick.

_____

_____

I made a spelling take when I wrote my story.

_____

_____

The little child behaved and got told off.

_____

_____

My dad was appointed when his football team lost.

_____

_____

My friend obeyed the teacher and lost her points.

_____

_____

I placed my homework and got into trouble at school.

_____

_____

Prefixes to make opposites

Some prefixes make a word mean the opposite. For lots of words you add **in** to a word, such as *visible – invisible*. However:

- if a word begins with the letter **r**, you use the prefix **ir** to change its meaning: *relevant – irrelevant*.
- if a word begins with the letter **l**, the prefix is **il**: *legible – illegible*.
- if a word begins with **m** or **p**, the prefix is **im**: *mature – immature*; *precise – imprecise*.

1. Add **in**, **il**, **ir** or **im** to these words to make their opposite meaning. Write them in the correct box in the table below.

> regular   legal   perfect   correct
> resistible   logical   patient   active

in	ir	il	im

2. Choose two of the words and write the meanings of the word without the prefix and with the prefix.

_____

_____

_____

_____

_____

The prefixes **in**, **il**, **im** and **ir** change words into their opposites.

3. **Which prefix would fit these words? Write each one with the correct prefix.**

accurate	_____
possible	_____
capable	_____
logical	_____
considerate	_____
regular	_____
dependent	_____
legal	_____
polite	_____
direct	_____
probable	_____
credible	_____

4. **in is probably the most popular prefix. List as many in words as you can.**

_____

_____

Rewrite your words with prefixes

The prefix **re** means *again* or *back*.
The prefix **inter** means *between* or *among*.

1. Add **re** or **inter** to these words to make new words.
   Write them in the correct boxes.

net   do   stellar   call   place   write   turn   act   national

re

inter

2. **The text below does not make sense. Decide which prefix, re or inter, needs to be added to each word in bold and write the new word below it.**

I had to **do** my homework because I could not **call** what my teacher told

_____

me to do. I had to **arrange** my paragraphs because they did not make

_____

sense and were not **connected**. I then had to **write** my paragraph about

_____

the **national** sports competition and say which countries were competing.

_____

I was working quite well until my brother **turned** and distracted me.

_____

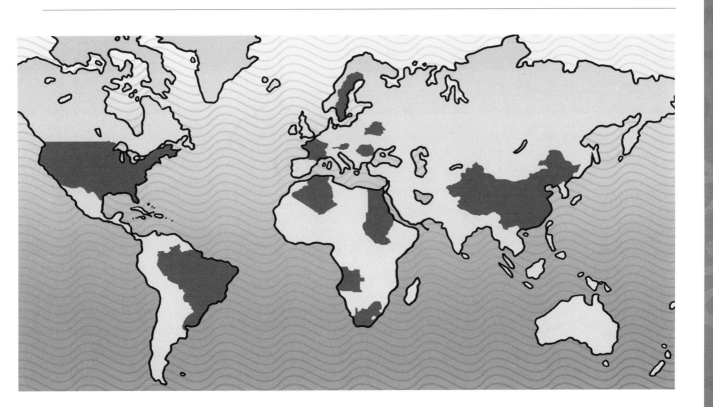

Super sub

The prefix **sub** means *under*.
The prefix **super** means *above*, *over* or *beyond*.

1. Add **super** or **sub** to each word and write it in the correct place. If you are not sure, try looking up your new word in the dictionary.

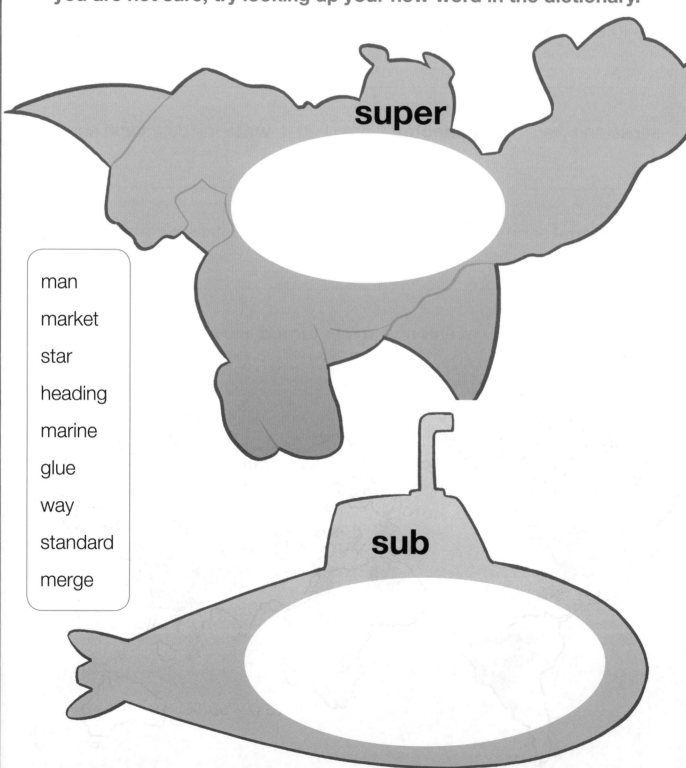

super

sub

man
market
star
heading
marine
glue
way
standard
merge

2. Write super in front of these words.

_____market

_____hero

_____sonic

3. Then write the super words beside their meanings.

A hero with more-than-ordinary powers. _____

A shop which is bigger than most. _____

Faster than the speed of sound. _____

4. Write sub in front of these words and then draw a line to the correct meaning.

_____marine   A tunnel under a road.

_____way   Less than 0.

_____merge   To put something under water.

_____zero   An underwater boat.

Anti and auto

The prefix **anti** means *against*.
The prefix **auto** means *self*.

1. **Add the prefix anti or auto to these words and then complete the table.**

> graph   clockwise   social   biography   virus
> septic   complete   biotic   freeze   mobile   pilot

anti	auto

2. The words below have their prefixes muddled up. Sort them out
   and write the correct spelling.

antigraph _____

autovirus _____

autolock _____

antimobile _____

autoclockwise _____

antipilot _____

autoseptic _____

antimatic _____

autosocial _____

autobiotic _____

3. Which word means *a signature* – especially of someone famous?

_____

Information about ation

Adding the suffix **ation** to a verb changes it into a noun.

- You just add **ation** if the word ends in a consonant: *inform – information*.
- If the word ends in **e**, take off the **e** before adding **ation**: *sense – sensation*.
- If the word ends in **ate**, take off the **ate** before adding **ation**: *accommodate – accommodation*.

1. Add **ation** to the words in the table.

Word	Word + ation
inform	*information*
accommodate	
admire	
sense	
prepare	
donate	
decorate	
cancel	
hesitate	

2. Find these words in the wordsearch. Tick each word as you find it.

☐ adoration ☐ donation ☐ information

☐ annotation ☐ formation ☐ preparation

☐ circulation

i	n	f	o	r	m	a	t	i	o	n	b	e	e	b	i	p	m
e	i	p	b	r	i	d	a	t	a	t	i	n	k	a	m	d	a
x	x	l	w	d	l	o	c	i	r	c	u	l	a	t	i	o	n
b	j	t	e	m	d	r	z	b	e	m	q	w	r	t	c	n	v
p	r	e	p	a	r	a	t	i	o	n	d	l	a	r	s	a	i
k	t	b	u	i	r	t	e	x	j	i	i	a	t	t	e	t	d
f	o	r	m	a	t	i	o	n	l	e	r	n	b	u	a	i	z
s	e	l	r	z	f	o	p	s	r	s	u	d	i	w	v	o	i
m	a	a	l	i	b	n	a	n	n	o	t	a	t	i	o	n	n

Usually ly

Adverbs are words which give more information about a verb. To make an adverb you can add the suffix **ly** to an adjective.

For most adjectives you just add the **ly** without adding or changing anything: *bad – badly*.

1. **Make some adverbs using the adjectives below. Write them in the spaces.**

   sad _____

   excited _____

   usual _____

   quiet _____

   jealous _____

   loud _____

2. **Now add the adverbs into the sentences below.**

   I am _____ noisy, but today I played _____.

   I am waiting _____ for the performance to begin.

   I _____ looked at my friend when she was playing with

   another child.

   The dog sat _____ as he couldn't go outside.

   I sang _____ in front of my friends.

If the adjective has more than one syllable and ends in **y**, change the **y** to **i** before adding **ly**: *happy – happily*.

3. Change these adjectives into adverbs following the rule.

    angry   _____

    bossy   _____

    funny   _____

    noisy   _____

    spooky   _____

If the adjective ends in **le**, change the **le** to **ly**: *gentle – gently*.

4. Change these adjectives into adverbs following this rule.

    adorable   _____

    simple   _____

    humble   _____

    noble   _____

    able   _____

5. Now choose two adverbs and write them in a sentence.

    _____

    _____

    _____

Spelling

The bold words in this story are adverbs.

When the monster rose up **angrily** from the canal we were very scared. We ran **quickly** to the police station and all started shouting **excitedly**. The policeman let us into the station and shut the door **abruptly**. The monster growled **loudly**.

6. **Write the root word for each adverb to find the adjective. The first one has been done for you.**

adverb	from adjective
angrily	angry

Basically al + ly

If the adjective ends in **ic**, then **al** is added before **ly**: *basic – basically*.

1. **Change these adjectives into adverbs following the rule.**

basic **basically**

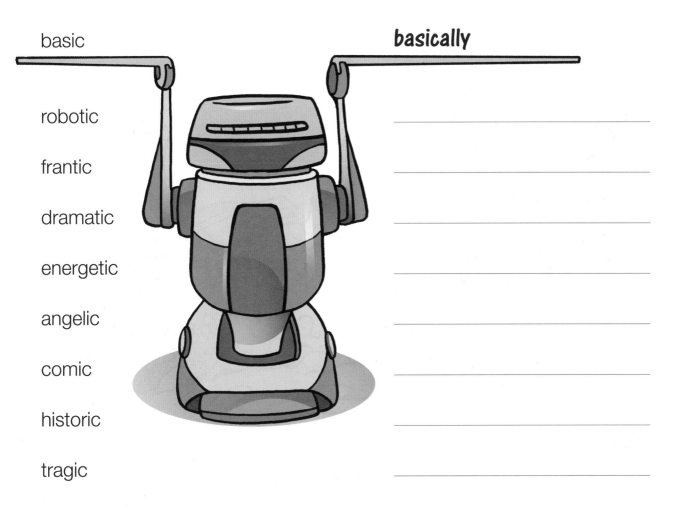

robotic _____

frantic _____

dramatic _____

energetic _____

angelic _____

comic _____

historic _____

tragic _____

2. **Now find the meanings of these words in a dictionary.**

3. **Find the adjectives that the adverbs** *truly*, *duly* **and** *wholly* **come from. Write down what you think the rule is to add ly to them.**

_____

_____

_____

Find the treasure

Words that end with the sounds **/zh/er/** are always spelled **sure**: *treasure*.

1. Find the **sure** words that belong in the treasure chest. Read the words on the coins and tick the coins that can go in the chest.

Words ending in ture

Words that end in the sound **/ch/er/** can be spelled **ture**.

1. Split the words into syllables and write the syllables in the balloons. The first one has been done for you.

Revision of division

When a word ends with the sound **/zh/u/n/**, it is always spelled **sion**: *division*. The ending **sion** is mostly added to words that end in **d**, **de** or **se**. Take off the **d**, **de** or **se** before adding **sion**.

1. **Add the sion endings to these words. The first one has been done for you.**

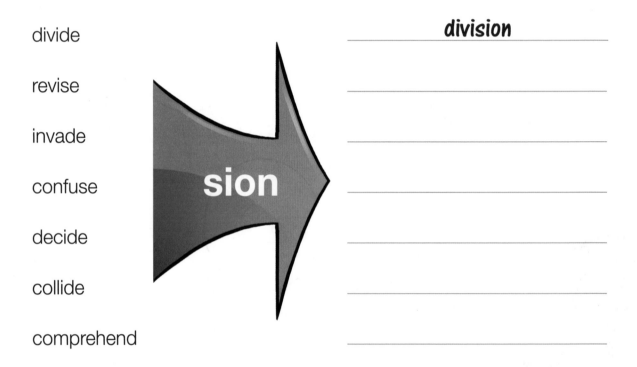

divide

revise

invade

confuse

sion

decide

collide

comprehend

_____ *division*

_____

_____

_____

_____

_____

_____

2. **Think of other words that have the ending sion and write them below.**

_____

_____

_____

_____

It's dangerous to add ous!

Adding **ous** to verbs or nouns makes adjectives. There are different rules for adding **ous**:

- Just add **ous**: *danger – dangerous*
- If a word ends in **our**, change it to **or** before adding **ous**: *humour – humorous*
- If the word ends with a **/j/** sound, keep the **e** before adding **ous**: *courageous*.

If there is an **/ee/** sound before the **ous** ending, it is usually spelled with an **i** (as in *serious*) but sometimes it is spelled with an **e** (as in *spontaneous*). Some words ending in **ous** have no obvious root word: *enormous, tremendous*.

1. Add **ous** to these words using the rules. Write the new words in the boxes.

prosper		poison	
courage		glamour	
humour		outrage	

2. Sort these **ous** words into the table below according to the rule they follow.

> tremendous serious hideous obvious jealous
> spontaneous courteous enormous hilarious

/ee/ sound before the **ous** ending, spelled with **i**	**/ee/** sound before the **ous** ending, spelled with an **e**	no **/ee/** sound and no obvious root word

Should it be tion or sion?

To decide on the correct spelling for a word with the sound **/sh/un/**, look at the root word.
- If it ends in **t** or **te**, take off the **t** or **te** and add **tion**: *inject – injection*.
- If it ends in **d**, **se** or **de**, take off the **d**, **se** or **de** and add **sion**: *expand – expansion*.

1. Join the words below with the correct suffix, **tion** or **sion**, and then write the new word. Make sure you remember the spelling rules for adding suffixes.

Word	Suffix	New word
adopt		_____
conclude		_____
invent	**tion**	_____
confuse		_____
complete		_____
obstruct		_____
explode	**sion**	_____
extend		_____

2. Which word means a thing that blocks something or someone's progress? _____

3. Which word means an ending? _____

ssion and cian endings

To decide on the correct spelling for a word with the sound **/sh/un/**, look at the root word.

- If it ends in **ss** or **mit**, take off the **ss** or **mit** and add **ssion**: *admit – admission*.
- If it ends in **c** or **cs**, take off the **c** or **cs** and add **cian**: *politics – politician*.

1. **Look at the root words below and then decide which word in the box has the correct spelling for the /sh/u/n/ sound. Circle the correct answer. The first one has been done for you.**

Root word	Option words	
express	exprecian	expression
confess	confession	confecian
optics	optission	optician
mathematics	mathematission	mathematician
admit	admician	admission
electric	electrician	electrission
transmit	transmician	transmission
music	musician	musission
magic	magission	magician
discuss	discucian	discussion

Which is it – tion, sion, ssion or cian?

Words which end with the sound **/sh/u/n/** can be spelled four different ways: **tion**, **sion**, **ssion** or **cian**. This depends on the spelling of the root word. Look back at pages 34 and 35 to remind yourself of the rules.

1. **Add tion, sion, ssion or cian to the words below using the rules you have learned.**

direct   _direction_

educate   _____

confess   _____

complete   _____

invent   _____

magic   _____

explode   _____

confuse   _____

electric   _____

extend   _____

permit   _____

express   _____

discuss   _____

music   _____

The echo sound

The letters **ch** can make the sound **/ch/**, as in *chocolate* or **/sh/**, as in *machine*.

In some words the letters **ch** make the sound **/k/**: *echo*.

1. **Read the words and underline those with the /k/ sound spelled ch.**

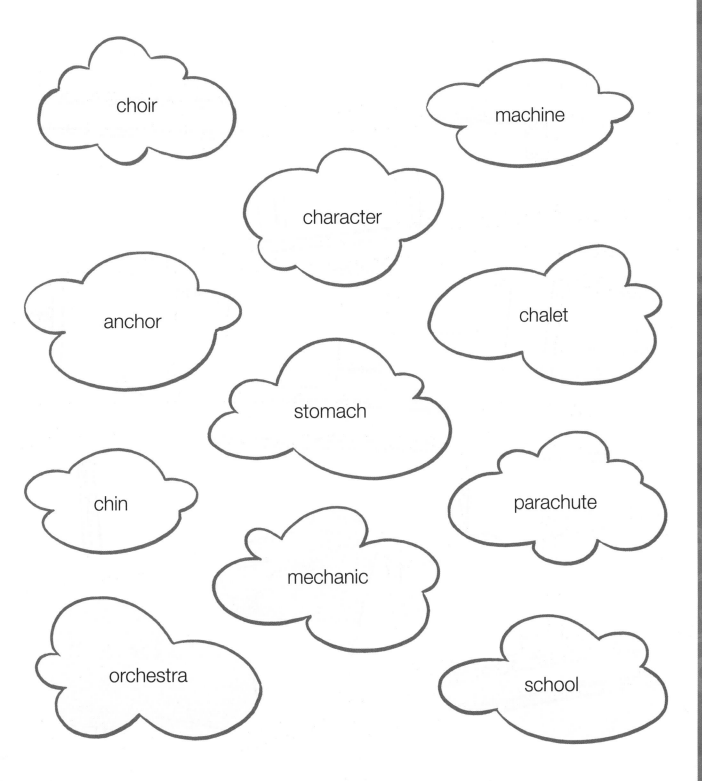

choir

machine

character

anchor

chalet

stomach

chin

parachute

mechanic

orchestra

school

The ch machine

In some words the letters **ch** make the sound **/sh/**: *machine*. Some French words that we use have this spelling for **/sh/**: *chef*.

1. Circle the words where the letters **ch** make the sound **/sh/**.

chain   chocolate   chin   brochure

school   such   chef   character   anchor

charade   stomach   chalet   parachute

champagne   mechanic

/sh/ sound

Plague and plaque

The word endings **gue** and **que** look quite similar. They make very different sounds:
- **gue** sounds like **/g/**: *plague*
- **que** sounds like **/k/**: *plaque*

Words that have the endings **gue** and **que** are mostly French words. In French, the letter **q** is pronounced **/k/**.

1. For each word, write the correct ending, **gue** or **que**. Then cover the word and try to rewrite it.

gue or que	Rewrite the word	gue or que	Rewrite the word
intri_____		lea_____	
ton_____		physi_____	
grotes_____		ro_____	
collea_____		uni_____	
opa_____		anti_____	
dialo_____		va_____	

2. Try and find out if all of these words are French. Write down the ones which are not and find the correct French word.

_____

_____

_____

Spelling

3. Look at these pictures. Decide which label is correct and write it underneath the picture.

labels

antique dialogue barbeque catalogue
cheque analogue tongue

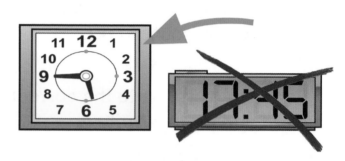

_____

_____

_____

_____

_____   _____   _____

The science of sc

In some words the sound **/s/** is made by the letters **sc**: *fascinate*.

1. **Complete the words by adding sc. Then draw a line to match each word to its meaning. Use a dictionary to help you.**

sc word	Meaning
de_____end	To go up.
_____ience	An implement to help you cut.
_____ene	A place where something happens: in real life, a book or a film.
_____issors	A curved shape which is wider in the centre than at the ends.
cre_____ent	The study of the physical and natural world.
a_____end	A smell.
_____ent	To go down.

Spelling

2. Find these words in the wordsearch. Tick each word as you find it.

- ☐ ascend
- ☐ scenery
- ☐ crescent
- ☐ scent
- ☐ descend
- ☐ science
- ☐ fascinate
- ☐ scientist
- ☐ scene
- ☐ scissors

s	c	i	e	n	c	e	e	a	d	f	w	k	o	e	t	d	b	e
c	z	a	f	x	b	s	c	n	e	s	j	t	m	w	e	o	s	l
e	n	v	m	u	p	b	e	l	s	c	e	n	e	r	y	a	p	p
n	r	l	e	v	l	c	d	f	c	i	p	i	y	u	r	r	k	c
e	t	s	p	u	s	t	d	p	e	s	r	e	h	c	e	j	a	l
q	g	h	g	a	c	e	t	a	n	s	c	i	e	n	t	i	s	t
c	r	e	s	c	e	n	t	m	d	o	v	g	x	o	g	u	v	a
w	l	s	m	l	n	e	w	a	z	r	e	x	a	t	m	n	a	e
d	l	u	f	q	t	h	v	f	a	s	c	i	n	a	t	e	h	b

3. Write other words that have the letters **sc** in them.

_____

_____

_____

How many ways of spelling /ai/?

The sound **/ai/** can be spelled as **a–e**, **ai** and **ay**. However, it can also be spelled **ei**, **eigh** and **ey**! There is no rule – they just have to be learned.

1. Correct these words. Use the clues to help you find out what they are. You can use the lines below to help you work out the correct spelling.

Word	Clue	Correct spelling
ayt	The number after 7.	_____
ospray	A bird of prey that eats fish.	_____
vayn	Something which carries around blood in your body.	_____
thai	When you describe lots of people without saying their names.	_____
obay	You need to do this to follow the rules.	_____
wai	Something you have to do with ingredients when making a cake.	_____
prai	You can go to a place of worship to do this.	_____
slai	You can travel in the snow on this.	_____
bage	A colour that is not quite brown.	_____

_____

_____

_____

Spelling

2. **Read this passage. Find the words that have the sound /ai/ spelled ei, eigh and ey and write them in the correct boxes below.**

I held the reins as we sat on the sleigh today. We were crossing a snowy field and saw large birds in the sky. They were circling over the lake looking for prey. My neighbour beside me shivered. The blood in my veins was getting cold too. The weight of the sleigh made it drag in the snow and the horses had to pull hard. The grey clouds got darker and it started to rain.

ei	eigh	ey

3. **Did you find any words that had the sound /ai/ but with a different spelling? Write them below.**

_____

_____

_____

It belongs to someone

Apostrophes are used to show that something belongs to someone or something: *The books belong to Jane – Jane's books.*

1. **Circle the correct use of the apostrophe, illustrated in the picture.**

the boy's bike

the boys bike's

the's boys bike

the gir'ls skateboard

the girl's skateboard

the girl' skateboard

Ad'am notebook

Adams notebook'

Adam's notebook

Lizzies' scooter

Lizzies scooter'

Lizzie's scooter

Mum's car

Mums' car

Mum car's

the dogs ba'll

the dog's ball

the dog' ball

How many dogs own the bone?

When you add an apostrophe to a noun to show possession, you add the apostrophe and then **s**: *the dog's bone*.

If the noun is plural and ends in **s** then you add just the apostrophe: *the dogs' bone*. This shows that the bone belongs to more than one dog.

1. **Change the singular nouns to plural nouns and add in the apostrophe correctly. The first one has been done for you.**

   The bird's nest   *The birds' nest* _____

   The boy's football team _____

   The horse's field _____

   My brother's room _____

   Her rabbit's cage _____

   The girl's classroom _____

Apostrophes

1. **Read these sentences and write in the missing apostrophes.**

   I cant believe I forgot my ticket – Ill just have to go back for it.

   I havent any choice – its lucky theres still enough time.

   A ducks eggs bigger than a hens egg, thats what I think.

   My umbrellas handles broken.

   Johns bike is off the road as its wheels tyres are flat.

   Its hundreds of miles from Lands End to John o Groats.

   This trees leaves have fallen off. Thats because its autumn.

   In summer I cant imagine winters snow, but last winter I couldnt imagine summers sunshine.

2. **Sort all the words with apostrophes in the sentences above in the correct box below.**

Abbreviations (shortened forms)	Possessives (to show ownership)
can't	duck's

Irregular plurals and apostrophes

Some plurals do not end in **s**: *child – children* it is an irregular noun.
To show possession for an irregular plural noun you add the apostrophe
and **s**: *child – children – children's*.

When a singular proper noun ends in **s** then you add the apostrophe and
the **s**: *Lewis – Lewis's*

1. **The sentences below have no apostrophes. Rewrite them, adding
   the possessive apostrophe in the correct place.**

The childrens playground was closed.

_____

James bike was left outside.

_____

The mices hole was in the wall.

_____

The mens race was in the afternoon.

_____

I like Cyprus beaches.

_____

Ellens house is on the corner.

_____

Homophones

Homophones are words that sound the same but have different spellings and different meanings.
For example:

- *to* is a common word that is used in lots of different ways including showing direction: *going to the cinema*, or before a verb: *to run*.
- *two* is the number 2
- *too* means *more than enough* or *as well*.

1. **Choose *to*, *two* or *too* to finish each sentence and write it in the space.**

The toddler was ☐ years old last week. We all went ☐

her birthday party. There were ☐ many people. I had ☐

helpings of ice cream! My brother enjoyed himself, and I did ☐ .

When the party was over we had ☐ go home.

2. **Choose *there*, *their* or *they're* to finish each sentence and write it in the space.**

My friends are over ☐ .

☐ all looking very smart.

☐ wearing ☐

best clothes. Where should they put

☐ things? Is ☐

a cloakroom downstairs?

Don't get mixed up between *there*, *their* and *they're*.

- *there* is a place word like *here*
- *their* means *belonging to them*
- *they're* is short for *they are*

Sounds the same

1. **Read the words in the box. Find the pairs of homophones and write them below.**

wail   dear   pair   fair   buy   fare   tale   know
by   meet   deer   whale   meat   no   pear   tail

_____   _____   _____   _____

_____   _____   _____   _____

_____   _____   _____   _____

_____   _____   _____   _____

2. **Look at your pairs of words and notice how the words are spelled. Underline the different letters that make the same sound.**

3. **Now write three sentences using some of these words. Make sure you choose the correct spelling!**

_____

_____

_____

_____

_____

_____

_____

Whether he spells it

1. Read the words in the box. Circle their homophones in the passage below.

bean   fare   sow   pear

I have been to the fair so I don't have any

money left. I ripped my jeans and had to sew

them up because I couldn't buy another pair.

2. Find the meanings of the words in the box and homophones you circled.

_____ _____

_____ _____

_____ _____

_____ _____

_____ _____

_____ _____

_____ _____

Meet or meat?

1. **Circle the correct word for these sentences.**

Akeem couldn't wait to **meet** / **meat** his friend, they were going to the zoo.

The cat got its **tale** / **tail** caught in the door.

Joseph has a long **wait** / **weight** for the bus.

Amy **mist** / **missed** the train.

The puppy hurt its **pour** / **poor** / **paw**.

"Could you **pour** / **poor** / **paw** the lemonade, please?"

Simon got a letter in the **mail** / **male**.

The **whether** / **weather** was awful so Maya couldn't play outside.

Phew, this is a heavy weight!

8 eight

2. **Choose one of the sentences. Think of ways to remember the different spellings of the words that sound the same. Write or draw your ideas below.**

Sounds like

1. Draw lines to match these homophones.

ball	hear
break	great
here	brake
grate	bawl

2. Choose two pairs of homophones and write a sentence to show the meaning of each word.

_____

_____

_____

_____

_____

_____

_____

_____

_____

_____

Spot the problem

1. **Read these sentences and think about why they don't make sense.
   Circle the homophone that is causing confusion and rewrite each
   sentence again using the correct word.**

I like to go to the park wear my sister is playing.

_____

_____

My mum likes to have some piece and quiet.

_____

_____

"We flew on a plain to get there," said Jacob.

_____

_____

"My, how you have groan!" said Nan.

_____

It was reigning outside.

_____

You will need sugar, butter, eggs and flower to make a cake.

_____

_____

Same sound – different meaning

1. Find the homophone of each word and write it in the box.

site

weak

male

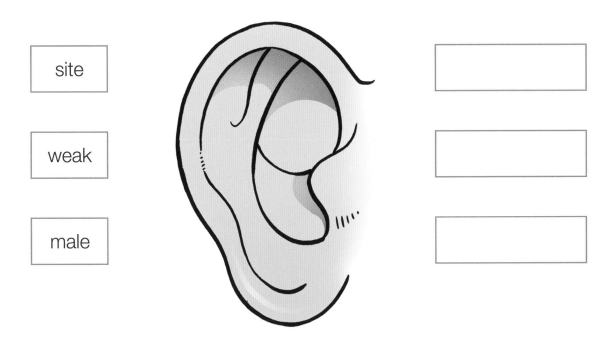

2. Write a sentence to show the meaning of each word.

Homophones crossword

1. Answer the clues to complete the crossword.

Clues across:

1. Today I know, yesterday

I __ __ __ __. (4)

4. Homophone of 2 down.

__ __ __ __ __ __ __ (7)

5. Homophone of 1 across.

__ __ __ (3)

7. Homophone of 1 down.

__ __ __ (3)

Clues down:

1. Tie two strings together with

a __ __ __ __. (4)

2. It's fun buying presents and

__ __ __ __ __ __ __ __

them up in coloured paper. (8)

3. Homophone of 6 down.

__ __ __ __ __ (5)

6. What you do with a pen to create

a letter: __ __ __ __ __. (5)

Creating nouns

A prefix is a group of letters that goes in front of words and changes the meaning of the word.

- **sub** means *under*
- **super** means *above*, *over* or *beyond*
- **anti** means *against*
- **auto** means *self*

1. **Add the correct prefixes to these nouns to create new nouns. Write their new meaning.**

> heading   biography   virus   hero   market

Prefix + word	Meaning
_____	_____
	_____
_____	_____
	_____
_____	_____
	_____
_____	_____
	_____

Creating more nouns

The prefix **inter** means *between* or *among*.
The prefix **bi** means *two*.
The prefix **tri** means *three*.

1. Add the prefixes above to these nouns to create new nouns.
   Use a dictionary if you do not know their new meanings.

Root word	Prefix + word	Meaning
national	_____	_____ _____
cycle	_____	_____ _____
angle	_____	_____ _____
city	_____	_____ _____
plane	_____	_____ _____

New nouns

tele means *at a distance*
trans means *across* or *beyond*
mini means *smaller than usual*

1. Match the words to the prefixes to create new nouns. Write the new nouns in the space on the right.

phone

bus

| trans |

vision

port

| tele |

former

| mini |

skirt

2. Find their new meanings in a dictionary and write them here.

Family trees

Word families are groups of words that are related in some way.

1. **Add the words below to the correct family trees. The first one has been started for you.**

medical   bicycle   recycle   medicine   unicycle   electricity   tricycle
electrical   electrician   electrify   medicate   medicinal

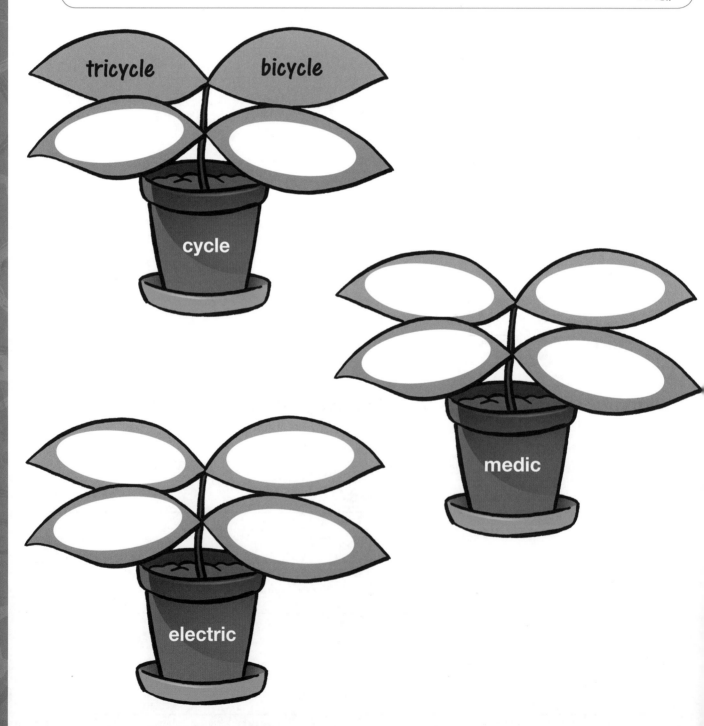

Cycle

The word *cycle* means something that goes round – this could be an event that is repeated or something which turns.

1. **Add these prefixes to the word *cycle* and then write their new meanings. Use the meaning of the word *cycle* to help you.**

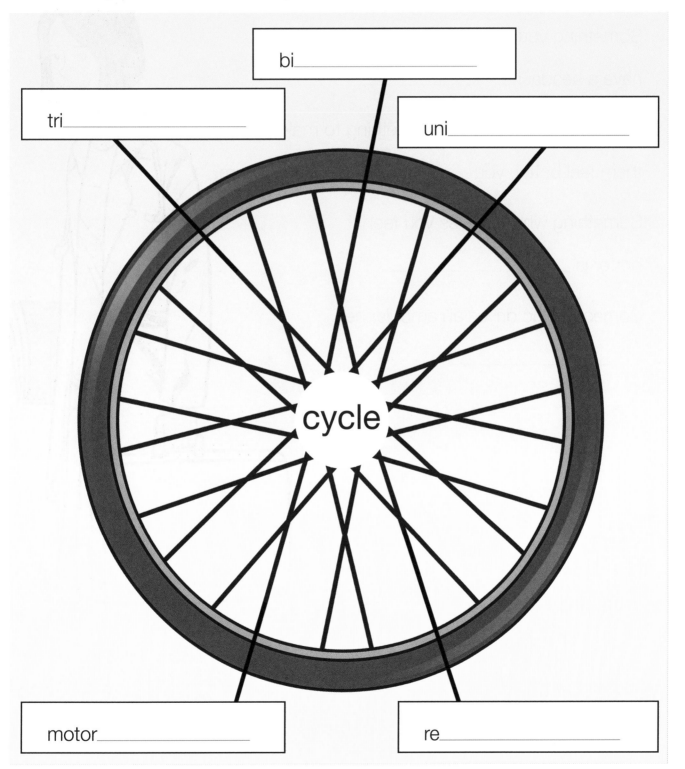

bi_____

tri_____

uni_____

cycle

motor_____

re_____

Medic

Medic is an informal name for a doctor. There are lots of words with *medic* in them.

1. **Match the clues and the words that belong to the *medic* word family together. Write the correct words in the spaces.**

   Something you might take if you

   have a headache. _____

   When you give someone something to make

   them feel better, you _____ them.

   Something which makes you feel

   better is _____.

   Someone who drives an ambulance.

   _____

   medicine
   medicinal
   medicate
   paramedic

2. **What links these words?**

   _____

   _____

A regular person

The word *regular* originally comes from Latin, meaning *a rule*. *Person* was originally a French word.

1. **Find words that belong to the *regular* and *person* family trees. Try to include one that has a prefix. Add them to the correct tree.**

regulation

personality

regular   person

2. **Look at one of the trees and write an explanation of what links the words.**

_____

_____

_____

Graphing

A graph is a diagram that shows information. However 'graph' is a suffix – or sometimes a prefix – which comes from the Greek word *graphos* which means *something drawn or written*.

1. **Find the meanings of the words below using the meaning of 'graph' to help you.**

   photograph _____

   _____

   telegraph _____

   _____

   grapheme _____

   _____

   autograph _____

   _____

   paragraph _____

   _____

2. **Think of other 'graph' words, or use a dictionary to find some. Write the words and their meanings below.**

   _____

   _____

   _____

Who did what?

A *pronoun* is a word which replaces a noun such as: *they, her, he, them, him, she, it*.

1. **Look at the pronouns above. Use them to replace the bold words in this passage.**

   The robber stole jewels and hid **the jewels** under his bed.

   _____

   The next day **the robber** looked for **the jewels**.

   _____

   "**The jewels** have gone!" **the robber** cried.

   _____

   "Do you mean that bag of junk?" said his mother. "I gave **the bag** to the police jumble sale."

   _____

   "Oh no!" said the robber, scowling at **his mother**.

   _____

   So **his mother** told **the robber** she was sorry.

   _____

Changing the nouns

Pronouns are used to avoid repeating nouns within a sentence. This helps to make writing easier to read.

1. **Rewrite these sentences. Use a pronoun so that the nouns are not repeated.**

There was a bird in my garden and the bird was building a nest.

_____

_____

Finlay wanted a banana because Finlay was hungry.

_____

_____

The man went swimming and then the man went for a run.

_____

_____

When Megan took Megan's dog, Arthur, for a walk, Megan tripped over Arthur because Megan was busy looking at Megan's mobile phone.

_____

_____

_____

Finding pronouns

1. **Improve this piece of writing by replacing most of the repeated names with pronouns. The first few have been done for you.**

John and Jenny

John and Jenny were best friends. ~~John~~ *He* always went around with

~~Jenny~~ *her*, and ~~Jenny~~ *she* never left ~~John~~ *him*. John and Jenny loved just playing

and chatting endlessly.

"Did John finish John's crisps? Give some to Jenny!" Jenny would

cry.

"John have none left," John would say sadly.

"What shall Jenny and John do now?" Jenny and John would often

wonder. "Let's hide so that no one will find Jenny and John."

So that is what Jenny and John did. Jenny and John would

disappear for hours and no one could find Jenny and John.

2. **Write the pronouns you have used in the boxes below.**

Being clear

If too many pronouns are used then it can make writing harder to read because it will not be clear who is doing the action or the talking. Read this passage:

My dad went to my uncle's house for dinner. He made him a cake and they ate it all.

Who made the cake? Was it the dad or the uncle? Now look at this passage:

My dad went to my uncle's house for dinner. He made my uncle a cake and they ate it all.

Who made the cake? It is clear that it was the dad.

1. **Rewrite these sentences to make it clear who is doing what.**

Jess took her homework to her friend's house. She helped her finish her story.

_____

_____

The boy jogged across the field with his friend. He fell and he helped him.

_____

_____

My friend wanted to go to the cinema. He asked him if he wanted to go with him.

_____

_____

Tense

The tense shows when the action in a sentence is taking place: the past or the present. It is the verb in the sentence which changes to show the tense.

The present tense shows what is happening now: *I **live** in London*.

The past tense shows what has happened: *I **lived** in London*. This suggests that I don't live there any longer.

If we want to describe what has been happening and is continuing to happen, we need to add another word to the verb in the sentence: *I **have lived** in London for four years*.

I could also say *I **was living** in London during the Olympic Games*. This suggests an action that started and finished in the past.

To write about the future, the verb in the sentence also uses another verb to show what will happen: *I **will live** in London when I am older*.

1. **Read these sentences and underline the word or words that show the tense. Use the clues in the box to help you.**

was + verb   *were* + verb   *will* + verb   *am* + verb   *is* + verb

Charlie ran to the shops.

The dog is barking at the cat.

I play in my room.

I will do my homework.

I am jumping over the bench.

I eat my food.

I will read that book.

They were going to the cinema.

The girl read her book.

I was singing in the choir.

I have done this

We sometimes add *has* or *have* before a verb to give more information about time and what has happened before.

Take the past-tense sentence: *Joe went out to play*. If the sentence is changed to *Joe **has gone** out to play*, the meaning has changed to suggest that Joe went out and is still out playing. Notice that as well as adding *has*, the verb form changed from *went* to *gone*.

If I say *When I got to the bus stop, the bus left*, it isn't clear whether I got on the bus in time or not. If I say *When I got to the bus stop, the bus **had left***, the words *had left* tell you that the bus left before I arrived.

1. Change these sentences by adding *has*, *had* or *have* before the verb. You many need to change the form of the verb as well. The first one has been done for you.

Ellie plays with her friend all day.

> **Ellie has played with her friend all day.**

Mum went to the shops.

James finished the marathon.

Olivia gave her game to her friend.

Ben saw the car in the garage.

Change the sentence

We sometimes add *has* or *have* before a verb to give more information about time and what has happened before: *took – has taken*; *went – has gone*; *looked – have looked*.

1. Change these sentences by adding *has* or *have* before the verb. You may need to change the form of the verb as well. The first one has been done for you.

I walked to school this morning.

   I have walked to school this morning.

I am skipping to my house.

_____

Edie took her recorder to school.

_____

I took the rubbish to the bin.

_____

My teacher left her bag in the classroom.

_____

I am playing in the football team.

_____

My dad was driving the car to the garage.

_____

Muddled sentences

1. The words in these sentences are in the wrong order. Rewrite them making sure you use *have* or *has* + verb correctly. Don't forget to start each new sentence with a capital letter.

---

this for a I have lived in house long time.

I have lived in this house for a long time.

---

cleaning John has the kitchen finished.

---

driven the woman shops has to the.

---

her my played sister has with friends.

---

my lost I have house keys.

---

finished the boy the has race.

Grace Darling

A conjunction links words and phrases together. For example: *Grace got in the boat **and** began to row.*

Some common conjunctions are: *and, if, so, while, though, since, when.*

1. **Read this true story about Grace Darling. Choose one of the conjunctions above to put in each gap below. You may use each conjunction in the list only once.**

On the morning of September 7, 1838, the steamer *Forfarshire*

was caught in a storm _____ she was on her way

to Liverpool. She hit a rock _____ began to sink. No

other lifeboat dared to risk the storm _____ Grace

and her father, William, put to sea in a small boat. They managed

to reach the wreck, _____ they could only rescue

five people in their small boat. _____ they reached

the shore, William, helped by two of the men, went to save four

others. However, _____ Grace had not been brave

enough to help her father on the first trip, all nine people would

have drowned. For her bravery, Grace was awarded a Gold

Medal, and so many people requested locks of her hair that she

joked that she had been almost bald _____ the rescue!

Grammar

Using conjunctions

1. **Find the sentences that go together. Rewrite them, using a conjunction to join them.**

because   or   so   when   but   if   as   while

Someone was lying in Grandma's bed.

She rushed out of the palace.

They could try to find their way home.

He could hear him snoring.

It didn't look like Grandma.

Jack knew the giant was sleeping.

Hansel and Gretel could wait for help.

Cinderella heard the clock strike midnight.

_____

_____

_____

_____

_____

_____

_____

_____

_____

_____

_____

Conjunctions

A conjunction can express time and cause within a sentence:

- *I cannot finish my homework* **because** *I haven't got a pen.*
  The word *because* is showing that the cause of not being able to finish the homework is not having a pen.
- *The boy cleaned his room* **before** *he went to play with his friend.*
  The word *before* tells us the time when he did the activities.

1. **Underline the conjunctions that express time or cause in these sentences. The first one has been done for you.**

I haven't been able to walk <u>since</u> I was ill.

The sun shone brightly after the rain stopped.

I ran after the dog when it took my ball.

While I went to watch television my brother played on the computer.

I wanted to see the film because all my friends had seen it.

My mother waited to make the cake until I got home.

She opened the door before the postman knocked.

As he had not arrived, the headteacher could not interview him.

Prepositions

A preposition shows us where something is, what time something happens or how something is being done: *The pen is **on** the table.* The preposition *on* tells us where the pen is.

Prepositions can link words together and can also express time and cause within a text:

- *My grandparents moved to this house **in** 2001.*
  Here, the preposition *in* is expressing time.
- *The doctor could find no reason **for** my stomach ache.*
  The preposition *for* is expressing a cause.

1. **Add the prepositions that express place, time or cause to complete the sentences.**

> to   by   during   at   in   after   due to   until

My homework has to be finished _____ Friday.

My dad will meet me _____ the swimming pool.

I'm going on holiday _____ a week.

The trip was cancelled _____ the weather.

I am not going _____ school today.

The class assembly was held _____ the afternoon.

_____ I finish this game, I will watch television.

I will be here _____ Tuesday.

Adverbs

Adverbs are words that help to give more information about a verb, an adjective or another adverb: *The girls walked **slowly**.*

An adverb can also express time and cause within a sentence:

- *I ran the first race and **then** pulled out of the second one.*
  The adverb *then* is expressing time.

- *I have not done my homework **therefore** I cannot go to the cinema.*
  The adverb *therefore* is expressing cause.

1. **Underline the adverbs that express time or cause.**

I always eat my apple with the skin.

The dog ran in the road and consequently caused a traffic jam.

I would like to go to back to my house soon.

Next, he ran into a shop and knocked over a table.

The boy has said he wants an orange now.

My sister has already left for school.

Afterwards, I am going to meet my friends.

Grammar

Time sequence

1. **Choose one of the words expressing time and cause to fill each gap in the text below. You may use each word or phrase once only.**

> meanwhile   after   again   first   because   during   so   when   soon

In 1066, Duke William landed at Hastings

_____

he believed he was King of England.

The

_____

thing he did was to order his cavalry to charge.

But the English axemen held them off

_____

the battle.

_____

the Normans were weakened and fled.

_____

the English saw this they ran after them.

But

_____

the English were surrounded and killed.

_____

this disaster, the English were badly weakened.

So the Normans attacked

_____.

King Harold was hit in the eye by an arrow. The battle was lost.

A dog, an orange

The first time something is mentioned, the word *a* is usually used: *The boy had* **a** *dog.* In some cases, the word *an* is used instead of *a*: *My sister rode on* **an** *elephant.* The use of *a* or *an* depends on the word that follows it:

- *a* is put in front of a noun beginning with a consonant: *a* **c***at*; *a* **s***hop*; *a* **t***ree*.
- *an* is put in front of a noun beginning with a vowel: *an* **o***wl*; *an* **a***ccident*; *an* **o***nion*.

1. **Decide whether *a* or *an* should go in front of each of these nouns.**

house

cat

umbrella

tree

bridge

a

apple

wall

mountain

egg

an

boy

friend

ice cream

uncle

coat

a house

Is it *a* or *an*?

If a noun begins with a consonant then the word *a* is used before it: *a bag*.

If there is also an adjective before the noun, the adjective affects whether *a* or *an* is used: *an **e**normous bag*. Here, the word *enormous* begins with a vowel and so *an* is used.

1. Complete these sentences using *a* or *an* correctly.

I ate _____ apple and _____ banana.

I saw _____ bag of flour on the shelf.

My mum saw _____ open packet of biscuits.

_____ horse was galloping in the field.

I ran in _____ race for my school.

Evie had _____ swollen ankle.

In a few cases, a word that begins with a vowel uses *a* instead of *an*: *a **u**nicorn* not *an **u**nicorn*. This is because the word *unicorn* begins with a **/y/** sound (the sound of a consonant) rather than the sound **/u/** (a vowel sound).

2. **Think of some more words that begin with vowels where *a* would be the correct word to use. Use them in a sentence below.**

_____

_____

_____

_____

Capitals and punctuation

A capital letter is used at the start of every sentence: **T**he boy went to bed.

Capital letters are used for proper nouns: My best friend is **J**ames.

If the sentence is a statement it ends in a full stop: My house is at the end of the street**.**

If the sentence is a question it ends in a question mark: Please can you help me**?**

If the sentence is an exclamation (perhaps something exciting, funny, angry or urgent) it ends in an exclamation mark: Run away**!**

1. These words and phrases need to be recycled into complete sentences. Rewrite them with the correct capital letters and end punctuation.

STOP
!?
CAPITAL
LETTER

covered with snow
look at me
down
ashley arrive
put the stick
when I'm talking to you
the mountain was
when will

Missing capital letters and punctuation

1. **King Capital has banned the use of capital letters. He has taken all the capital letters out of these two pieces of writing. Can you put them back?**

mrs higgins and her red umbrella

suddenly the wind blew. it took mrs higgins and her umbrella

up, up, up into the sky! over park lane school she flew. over mr

jackson's house… over scott street… over buttercup farm… over

the hills and far away.

"help!" screamed mrs higgins, as loud as she could. "help!"

my diary

friday

we went to cromwell street library today. i got a book
about the planet mars. it's called *amazing mars*.

saturday

i am going to ben h's party. sam, adam and ben w are
going as well.

it will be great!

sunday

oldbury rovers won 5–0! wow!

Capital news

1. Find and correct all the missing capital letters in this newspaper article. One has been done for you.

"do you believe in fairies?" asks bogsworth echo chief reporter, helen doughty

F̶or centuries fairies have been put at risk through the danger of human disbelief in their existence. now fairy lovers and pixie protectors have joined forces to form a society to protect the little people. the we believe in fairies society (webifs) plan to change people's perception of fairyland.

"they're not just something from story books," said june thistledown. "we aim to make people believe in fairies so that they can be preserved."

if you want to join the webifs, the next meeting will be in bogsworth guildhall at 7pm on wednesday 5th july.

the chairperson of the webifs, robin small, added, "on sunday we will be heading down dingly lane to see if we can spot any fairies in dingly wood. anyone wishing to come should bring their own toadstool and a bag to collect fairy dust."

the group has the support of dingly woodland trust, which owns and manages the forest. bagsworth council is also keen to get involved. indeed, the society has attracted extra visitors to bagsworth wood and it seems that local people are keen to spot a fairy. however, our photographer was unable to find any fairy folk in the forest. it may be that all the publicity has frightened them away.

Punctuation

Is it *it's* or *its*?

Apostrophes can be used to show a letter is missing. Remember that **it's** (with an apostrophe) stands for **it is** while **its** (without an apostrophe) is to do with belonging.

1. Choose the right *it's* or *its* to fill each space.

_____ a beautiful day. The sun is shining in all _____ glory. Just listen

to the blackbird singing _____ heart out up on _____ high perch in the

park. Down below sits the cat minding _____ own business. _____ just

lazing in the sun, licking _____ paws from time to time. For once _____

not raining!

_____ a pity then, that we are stuck indoors. The school – with _____

teachers, children and all _____ other staff – has _____ work to do.

_____ a very busy place. School has _____ up and _____ downs.

Never mind, _____ often fun and _____ got _____ pleasures too – like

sorting out whether _____ '_____' or '_____'! Or would you rather be

in the park with the blackbird singing _____ song?

Jason's lipstick

The apostrophe can be used to show ownership: *Molly's mobile phone was broken. Tom stole Harry's book.*

1. Match each owner to an object and write a sentence about them, including an apostrophe to show ownership. The first one has been done for you.

Jason	Priti	car	kennel

Mr Smith	The policeman	space ship	handcuffs

Rover	The alien	lipstick	bicycle

Jason's lipstick was purple.

Does it belong to her or them?

When you add an apostrophe to a noun to show possession, you add the apostrophe and then **s**: *the bird's nest*. In this sentence, one bird owns the nest.

If the noun is plural and ends in **s** then you add just the apostrophe: *the birds' nest*. In this sentence, the nest belongs to more than one bird.

1. **Change these singular nouns to plural nouns.**

dog _____   player _____

week _____   boy _____

snake _____   girl _____

friend _____   dragon _____

2. **Write sentences which show ownership using each of the plural nouns. One has been done for you.**

I need to finish my homework in two weeks' time.

_____

_____

_____

_____

_____

_____

_____

Irregular plural apostrophe

The plural of *child* is *children*, an irregular plural noun. To show possession for an irregular plural noun you add the apostrophe and **s**: *child – children – children's*.

1. Draw a line to match the singular nouns to the plural nouns.

goose	mice
mouse	men
person	women
woman	people
man	geese

2. Now add apostrophe and **s** to the plural nouns and complete the sentences below.

The _____ pond is on the farm.

The _____ changing room is at the pool.

The _____ cheese is on the floor.

The _____ palace is in the city.

The _____ football team is practising.

Hot sleepysaurus

In the sentence *Mum said that we were not going to the fair today*, it is not clear exactly what Mum said. In order to show the exact words that were said, inverted commas are used: *"We are not going to the fair today," said Mum.* They are put around the words that are spoken and are also known as *speech marks*.

1. **Highlight all the inverted commas in this story and then read it aloud.**

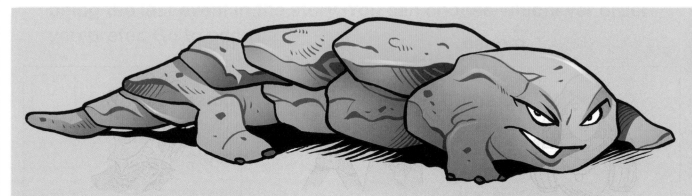

The Sleepysaurus is a creature like a rock garden that turns up at Bell Street Flats. This is what happened when it began to get too hot:

The Sleepysaurus lay there in the sun getting hotter and hotter, and we all thought a lot.

"We can't carry baths," said Niki.

"And the Mean Man has taken away the hose pipe," said Rashid. "What about buckets?" I said.

We got our buckets, and then we looked at the Sleepysaurus. "How many bucketfuls do we need?" I asked Rashid and Niki. "Hundreds!" said Rashid.

"Thousands!" said Niki. "Millions!" I said. "Billions!" said Rashid. "Trillions!" said Niki.

"Hundreds of thousands of millions of billions of trillions!" I said. "And there's only one tap in the yard!"

from *Our Sleepysaurus* © 1988 Martin Waddell

Speech marks

1. Add speech marks to the passage to show what the characters said.

Soon Second Little Pig met a woodcutter.

Hello Mr Woodcutter, said Second Little Pig, You have got a great big pile of sticks here. Can you spare some for me?

Certainly. What do you want sticks for? asked the woodcutter.

I am going to build a lovely warm house to live in, boasted Second Little Pig.

Later, Third Little Pig met a man who was making bricks.

Hello Mr Brick-maker, said Third Little Pig.

Hello Little Pig, answered the brick-maker, Where are you off to today?

I am going to build a good strong house to live in. Will you let me have some of your bricks?

That's a good idea, said the brick-maker. Bricks make strong houses, he added.

Direct speech

Inverted commas appear at the beginning and end of the words that characters say: *The Giant shouted "Fee, fi, fo fum!" Jack replied "You will never catch me."*

When speech is written in a story or report, a phrase before or after is usually used to introduce it. This tells us who said the words. Some examples are: *he said, she replied, Mum cried, the boy yelled, Dad asked, the girl whispered.*

1. **Look at this scene. Write the words each character is saying inside the inverted commas.**

Father Bear asked,

" _____

_____ ?"

" _____

_____ ?"

Baby Bear cried.

2. **Now write what happens in this scene. Remember to write who is speaking and to put their words in inverted commas.**

_____

_____

_____

_____

What are they saying?

1. **Look at the picture of Mum, Jack and Freya. Write what each person says using inverted commas. Remember to use a phrase to show who is speaking.**

_____

_____

_____

_____

_____

_____

The choosing

The *theme* of a story is the subject or idea that it is about. Stories can have many different themes. Traditional stories often have the theme of good versus evil, where a good character suffers, but finally defeats the evil character and lives happily ever after.

The theme of the story below is making choices. Read the story and then answer the questions.

There was once a young shepherd who wished to marry. He knew three sisters who were all equally lovely, so it was difficult for him to choose between them.

So he asked his mother for advice. She said, "Invite all three to our house and put some cheese on the table before them. Then watch how they eat it."

Next day, the young man invited the three sisters to his house and put a plate of cheese in front of each one. The first girl swallowed the cheese with the rind on. The second girl hastily cut the rind off the cheese, but she cut it so quickly that she left much good cheese with it, and threw that away as well. The third girl, however, peeled the rind off carefully, and wasted none of the cheese.

The young man asked his mother what she thought of the three girls. She replied, "Take the third for your wife."

This he did, and lived contentedly and happily with her.

The Brothers Grimm

1. **Why did the shepherd find it difficult to choose between the three sisters?**

_____

_____

_____

2. **What did the way they ate the cheese show about them?**

_____

_____

_____

3. **How do you think the shepherd should have found the most suitable girl?**

_____

_____

_____

4. **What kind of a wife do you think the third girl will be?**

_____

_____

_____

Writing charts from text

1. **Read the descriptions of the horse and the goat on this page and the next one. Then fill in the chart on the next page with some key facts. Just write notes about the key facts, the information that you are being asked to find. For example, if you were asked where the goat lives you would write *shed* not *the goat lives in a smelly shed*.**

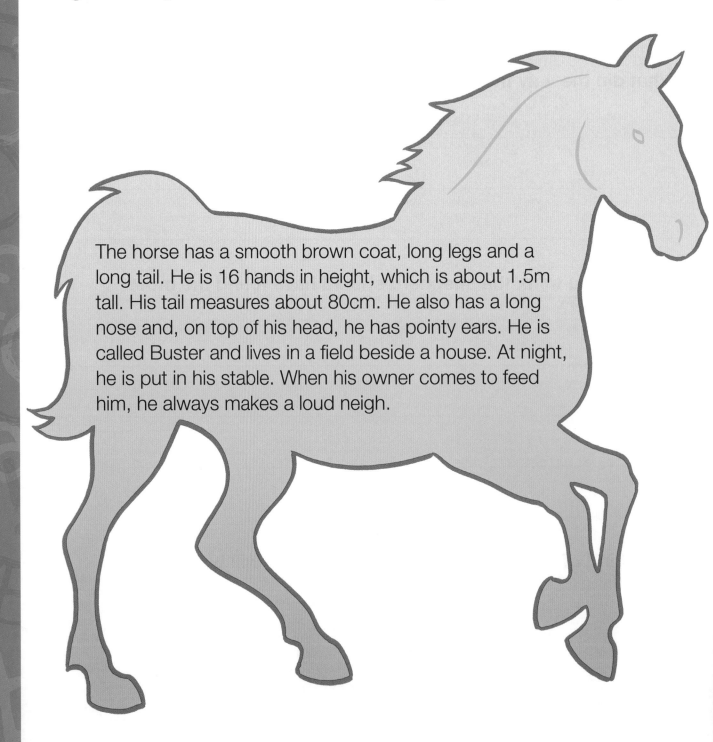

The horse has a smooth brown coat, long legs and a long tail. He is 16 hands in height, which is about 1.5m tall. His tail measures about 80cm. He also has a long nose and, on top of his head, he has pointy ears. He is called Buster and lives in a field beside a house. At night, he is put in his stable. When his owner comes to feed him, he always makes a loud neigh.

The goat lives in a smelly shed with a bed of straw on the floor. His name is Grumpy and he likes to kick and bleat at people. He is about 90cm tall, has grey fur, short legs and a short stumpy tail, which is about 10cm. He eats all the time and often gets his head stuck in between the fence wire.

	Horse	Goat
Home		
Colour		
Sleeping place		
Sounds		
Size of tail		
Height		

I had a boat

One of these of poems is a rhyming poem and the other is a non-rhyming poem. Say which is which, then examine the way they are set out.

I had a boat, and the boat had wings;
And I dreamed that we went flying
Over the heads of queens and kings,
Over the souls of dead and dying,
Up among the stars and the great white rings,
And where the Moon on her back is lying.

Mary Coleridge

My boat is my escape
I push it out
onto the lake
and lie back
and look at the sky
and I feel I am
floating up there
far away
from my problems

Amy Reeves

There are many different types of poem:

- *free verse* – a poem that doesn't follow any rules about rhyming or how to write it.
- *haiku* – a poem that follows strict rules of using only three lines and only using words which make up five syllables on the first and last lines and seven on the middle line.
- *acrostic* – a poem that uses the letters of a word that the poem is about as the start of each line.
- *shape poem* – the words in these poems make the shape of what the poem is about.

Some of these poems rhyme and some do not. Some of the rhymes are at the end of every line, some are every other line and some can have rhyming pairs of lines. It depends what the poet wants to do.

Read the poems on page 96 and answer the questions below.

1. Which poem rhymes?

_____

Does it rhyme on every line? If not, then how does it rhyme?

_____

_____

2. What type of poem is the second poem? Look at the types listed above.

_____

3. Both poems talk about going up in the sky. Why do you think this is?

_____

Dinosaur key facts

Read this text about dinosaurs and answer the questions on page 99.

There was a time when dinosaurs roamed the earth and were the main species on the planet. There were many different types of dinosaur and they were all sorts of shapes and sizes. The most fierce dinosaur was Tyrannosaurus rex. It was about 12m long and 6m tall. Other dinosaurs were very small; Composagnathus is the smallest dinosaur that has so far been discovered and was about the same size as a chicken.

Other reptiles which were related to dinosaurs flew. Many scientists think they were the distant ancestors of modern birds. Some dinosaurs could swim but none of them actually lived in water. However, there were other reptiles at the time of the dinosaurs that lived in water.

The last dinosaurs died out 65 million years ago. No one knows for certain why the dinosaur age came to an end. The most accepted cause is that an asteroid hit the earth and caused a great change in climate. The dinosaurs could not adapt to the changes and so became extinct.

The text on page 98 is a non-fiction text about dinosaurs. It contains information about dinosaurs such as what they looked like and when they lived. The information gives us key facts about dinosaurs. In the first paragraph, the key facts have been underlined. These key facts just contain the words which give us the information about dinosaurs and not every word in the sentence. Use the key facts to answer the questions below.

1. Which dinosaur was the most fierce?

_____

2. Which dinosaur was the smallest?

_____

3. How tall was the Tyrannosaurus rex?

_____

Re-read the second and third paragraphs. Find and underline the key facts. Then use the keys facts to answer the questions below.

4. Do scientists think that dinosaurs are the ancestors of modern-day birds? Y ☐ N ☐

5. Did dinosaurs live in water? Y ☐ N ☐

6. When did the last dinosaur die out?

_____

7. What does *extinct* mean?

_____

The Mousehole Cat

Read the text then answer the questions on page 101.

Then one year there came a terrible winter. At the far end of England the blue-green sea turned grey and black.

The Great Storm Cat is stirring, thought Mowzer as she watched at her window. The wind howled like a wild thing about the high headlands. It came hunting the fishing boats in their hidden harbours. When the Great Storm Cat is howling, thought Mowzer, it is best to stay indoors by a friendly fire.

The sea drew itself up into giant waves and flung itself against the great breakwaters. All along the coast of Cornwall, the stone walls stood the shock.

Then the sea sucked up its strength again and roared right over them, sinking the sailing boats in their home havens. But it could not get into the Mousehole.

Mowzer watched as the Great Storm Cat clawed with his giant cat's paw through the gap in the harbour wall. But it was too small.

He snarled and leaped up at the great breakwater under the lowering sky. But it was too high.

The fishing boats sat safe as mice in their own mousehole. But they could not get out.

There are different things to think about when you read or write a story:

- The *setting* is where the character(s) in the story live, play, work etc.
- The *plot* is the main events of the story: what happens to your character, what problems they encounter and how they solve them.

Read the text on page 100 then answer the questions below. The questions look at the setting and plot of the story.

1. Tick which setting fits the story.

☐ at the seaside ☐ in the mountains ☐ in the desert

2. Draw a line from each word to its meaning. (Look them up in a dictionary if you don't know.)

headland   a place to be safe or to rest

breakwater   a narrow bit of land extending out into the sea

haven   a wall surrounding a harbour to protect the
                                  boats from stormy weather

3. Which words and phrases describe the storm? One has been done for you.

howled

4. Why do you think the author uses the word *mousehole* when describing the harbour?

5. Where do you think this extract comes in the story?

☐ beginning ☐ middle ☐ end

Crabs

Read this passage about crabs. Highlight five facts that you think are important. Then rewrite your five facts in one paragraph.

Crabs are related to lobsters and shrimps. They have five pairs of legs, the first pair having claws. The other four pairs are used for walking, which most crabs do by moving sideways. Most crabs have hard shells, though the hermit crab does not grow a shell of its own. It has to find one on the sea-bed.

Crabs come in all sizes. The smallest are pea crabs, which are like tiny insects. The largest are Japanese spider crabs, which may measure up to 3·5 metres from tip to tip of their outstretched claws.

Some types of crab eat vegetables, some catch live animals, but most crabs find their food by scavenging, in other words by searching around for scraps of dead or decaying matter.

Crabs lay eggs, and their young have to shed their shell every time they get larger and grow a new one.

Crabs live for between 3 and 12 years.

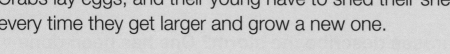

Seaside index

An index is a detailed alphabetical list of all the topics in a book.

People's names are written with the last name first.

Articles such as *a* and *the* are written after the main word.

When a range of pages is listed, for example 5–7, this is the place where the most information about a topic can be found.

Look at the index and time yourself on the tasks below.

A
Antarctica 2, 5, 18, 20, 30–1
Arctic, the 31
arctic tern 32

B
barnacle 15
blenny 19
Bounty, HMS 23
butterfish 17

C
clam 12,15
Cook, Captain James 27
coral 25
crab 8, 9–11, 28
Crusoe, Robinson 26

E
eel 2, 5–6
eskimo 4, 30

F
fish 17, 19–21, 29
flatfish 19
flounder 20
fossil 18, 30

L
limpet 23
lobster 5
lugworm 21

P
pearl 3, 7
penguin 31
polar bear 32
puffin 30

R
razorbill 14
rockling 22
rockpool 7, 9, 29

S
sand dunes 15
scallop 9
sea anemone 24
seals 8
seaweed 31
Scott, Robert F 27, 30
shell 4,11, 22
shingle 5
starfish 11

1. **Where would you look to find out about polar bears?**

_____

2. **Which page gives information about Captain Cook?**

_____

3. **In which pages would you find most information about fish?**

_____

Every game's a home game with my footy family

Grandad's in the goal
Dad's in defence
Mother's in midfield
Baby's on the bench

Sister's centre forward
Brother's at the back
Cousin is the coach
Auntie's in attack

Nana is the manager
and just because I missed
a penalty last home match
I'm on the transfer list.

Paul Cookson

Read the poem on page 104 and answer the questions below.

1. What is the poem about?

_____

2. Is the poem serious or light-hearted?

_____

3. Find and write the rhyming words in each verse.

_____

_____

4. What do you notice about the beginning sounds of the important words on each line in verse 1?

_____

5. *Alliteration* means words starting with the same sounds such as *dad* and *defence*. Find and write down the alliterative words in verse 2.

_____

_____

6. What is different about the way the poet has written the last verse?

_____

Comprehension

Midnight for Charlie Bone

Read the text and then answer the questions on page 107.

With tears and kisses from Maisie, a wave from Paton and a grim smile from Grandma Bone, Charlie and his mother were bundled into the taxi. They were dropped off in a side road leading to the academy, and then walked through a medieval square where cobblestones surrounded a fountain of stone swans. Ahead was a tall grey building, ancient and imposing. The walls that flanked the square were five storeys high, their windows dark rectangles of reflecting glass.

On either side of the huge arched entrance, there was a tall tower with a pointed roof, and when they reached the wide flight of steps up to the entrance, Charlie's mother suddenly stopped and stared up at a window in one of the towers. Her face was drained of colour and, for a moment, Charlie thought she was going to faint.

Answer the questions below and on page 107 about the text above.

1. **Which type of transport do Charlie and his mum use? Tick the correct answer.**

   ☐ car   ☐ taxi   ☐ bus

2. **What does *bundled* mean in line 2?**

   _____

3. **Which words in the first sentence describe how the characters are feeling?**

   _____

4. **Where are Charlie and his mum going? Tick your answer.**

  ☐ hospital   ☐ school   ☐ theatre

  Which word is used to tell you where they are going?

_____

5. **Find these words about size in the text. How do they help to describe the setting of the story?**

> tall   five storeys high   huge   wide

_____

_____

6. **Summarise what has happened in the story. Write one or two sentences.**

_____

_____

7. **Where do you think this extract comes in the story? Tick the correct answer.**

  ☐ beginning   ☐ middle   ☐ end

8. **What do the words *drained of colour* mean in the last sentence?**

_____

_____

Why?

Perform this poem with another person. Then, on a separate sheet, add more verses following the same pattern. A good place to add the new verses would be before the last two lines.

Read this poem and then answer the questions on page 109.

I'm just going out for a moment

I'm just going out for a moment.
Why?
To make a cup of tea.
Why?
Because I'm thirsty.
Why?
Because it's hot.
Why?
Because the sun is shining.
Why?
Because it's summer.
Why?
Because that's when it is.
Why?
Why don't you stop saying why?
Why?

Michael Rosen

Answer these questions about the poem on page 108.

1. What is the person going out to do?

_____

2. Why is it hot?

_____

3. Why do you think the poet wrote this poem and repeated the word *why*?

_____

_____

4. Do you think it is a funny or a serious poem?

_____

5. Is this poem free verse or one that follows rules?

_____

6. Write another verse using a different starting statement such as *I am going to go to the shops.* Try to match the style of the poem, for example by using repetition and questions.

_____

_____

_____

_____

Solids, liquids and gases

Read this text and then answer the questions on page 111.

All materials are either solids, liquids or gases. Solids keep their own shape. They can be hard, like wood, or soft, like bread.

Materials can turn from solids to liquids and from liquids to gases. It often depends on the temperature. Water runs out of the tap as a liquid.

But if we make water cold enough, it freezes into a solid – ice.

If we warm the ice, it melts back to water.

Liquids take the shape of their container. If you pour a liquid, it will run. Some liquids are sticky and run more slowly.

If we heat water until it boils, it turns into a gas – steam. We call this change evaporation.

Gases don't even stay in their container, unless it is completely sealed. If they escape, they spread out all over the room.

If we let steam cool, it turns back into a liquid. We call this change condensation.

Answer these questions about the explanation text on page 110.

1. Is this fiction or non-fiction? _____

2. What is a solid? _____

3. What is a liquid? _____

4. What is a gas? _____

5. What does *condensation* mean?

   _____

6. What does *evaporation* mean?

   _____

Read the text again and complete the table.

Does the text have...	Tick or cross	Example
headings or subheadings?		
verbs in the past tense? (*changed*)		
verbs in the present tense? (*change*)		
words expressing cause? (*because*)		
topic words? (*liquids*)		
illustrations?		

The Ant and the Grasshopper

Look at the picture. Which piece of writing do you think would be easier to read?

Paragraphs are groups of sentences. They help to structure your writing, making it easier to read.

A paragraph usually has one main point or overall idea. A paragraph is used to group related information to show a new, or the next, step in the writing.

A new paragraph starts on a new line and is often *indented* (starts to the right of the main text). Some books use a line space between paragraphs.

Read the story *The Ant and the Grasshopper* in the left-hand column of the table and then read the main points of each paragraph in the right-hand column. The story continues on the next page.

Story paragraphs	Main points
One fine summer's day, a grasshopper was hopping about in a field, chirping and singing to its heart's content. After a while, an ant struggled by, carrying a huge corn cob to his nest.	It is summer and Grasshopper is playing and an ant is working hard.
Grasshopper asked the ant to come and play with him rather than work so hard on this fine day. But Ant said he was helping to store more food for the winter and that if Grasshopper was wise he should do the same.	Grasshopper doesn't understand why Ant is working and Ant says that he is storing food for the winter.

1. **Read the end of the story and look at the main points. Write the missing paragraph at the end using the main points to help you.**

Story paragraphs	Main points
Grasshopper laughed at Ant. He pointed at the countryside around and at all the food in the trees and fields. He told Ant that there was more than enough food and that winter was such a long time away. Grasshopper wanted Ant to sing and dance, not waste time collecting food.	Grasshopper thinks this is funny and thinks there is lots of food. He wants to dance and sing, not work.
Ant shook his head and took up his heavy load again. Backwards and forwards he went, all day, with one heavy load after another while Grasshopper played.	Ant works hard collecting the food as Grasshopper plays.
_____	The winter comes and Grasshopper is starving while the ants are eating their stored food. Wise old saying: 'It is wise to prepare for hard times.'

Puppy problem

A writer has started planning a story. She has written the first sentence of each paragraph. The right-hand column explains what each paragraph will be about.

1. **Finish writing the paragraphs, using the questions in brackets to help you. The story continues on the next page.**

Sam was a new puppy who had just come to live in Lucy's house.

_____

_____

_____

_____

This paragraph describes Sam. (What did Sam look like? What games did he play?)

Sam liked living in Lucy's house but he kept getting into trouble.

_____

_____

_____

_____

This paragraph describes what Sam did. (What did he do wrong? What did he do to get into trouble?)

Then one day Lucy said, "You will have to go to school to be trained!"

_____

_____

_____

_____

This paragraph describes how Sam was trained. (What types of activity did he learn, such as how to sit?)

2. **Finish writing the paragraphs, using the questions in brackets to help you. Look back at page 114 if you need to.**

When he had finished at school, Sam knew how to behave.

_____

_____

_____

_____

> *This paragraph describes how Sam changed after dog school.*
> *(What was he like afterwards? Did he still get into trouble?)*

After that, Sam managed to keep out of trouble – well most of the time!

3. **Write about an adventure that Sam the puppy has. Use three paragraphs to describe the adventure and remember to keep one main idea in each paragraph. You can use one of the ideas below or make up your own.**

Sam is lost	**Paragraphs**
	Sam wanders off
	Lucy realises
	Sam is found

Sam at the park	**Paragraphs**
	Sam runs after a ball
	Sam falls into the pond
	Sam is saved by a boy

_____

_____

_____

_____

_____

Creating characters

When you plan a story it is important to plan your characters. The characters are who your story is about. Your characters will also help you plan your setting and your plot.

1. **Answer the questions below about this character.**

What is the character wearing?

_____

How is he standing?

_____

Does he look happy or sad?

_____

What colour is his hair?

_____

What else do you notice about him?

_____

2. **Now think about what you can't see in the picture. Write your ideas for each question below. The questions continue on page 117.**

    What is the character's personality like – are they funny or miserable? Why?

    _____

    _____

    _____

Where does the character live and why do they live there?

_____

_____

What are they doing now?

_____

_____

What might happen to them?

_____

_____

3. **Look back at your answer to the last question *What might happen to them?* Think about what the character would be thinking or feeling at a key point in this event. Now imagine what the character would say. Write his words on the lines below. Remember that it is the character who is speaking, so you should use 'I' in the speech.**

_____

_____

_____

_____

_____

_____

_____

Picture the setting

Planning the settings of your story is important. It might be that you start your story from a setting and then think of the characters that live there. However, you might have already decided on your character and have chosen where they live and where they will go.

When you plan your settings ask yourself the question: What can your character see, smell or hear? This will start to create a picture of the settings. If they hear birds and see fields then they might be in the countryside.

Think about the weather. A story set in the mountains might have snowy weather, whereas a story set at the beach might have sunny weather.

1. **Look at the settings below and choose one to write about. Circle your choice, then go to page 119.**

Outer space
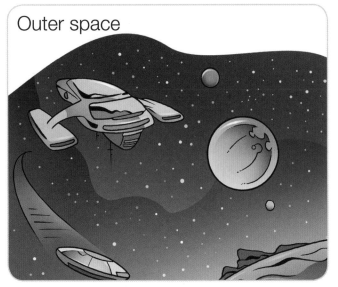

Enchanted castle

Deserted house

School
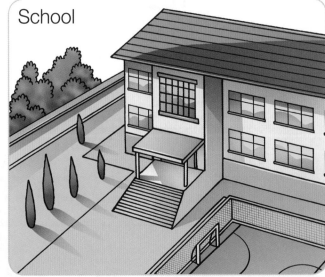

2. Choose a picture from page 118 and use the planning frame below to plan your setting. List words and draw ideas in the other boxes.

sounds	weather

smells	objects	colours

3. Use your notes and ideas to help you write a description of your setting. Include lots of detail.

_____

_____

_____

_____

_____

_____

Robin Hood plot

The plot describes what happens to your character at the beginning, middle and end of the story. The plot describes the main events in the story, the problems your character faces and how they resolve them.

1. **Look at these pictures and read about the main events from the Robin Hood story. Decide which event comes first and write the number 1 in the box. Then carry on ordering events, with number 9 being the last event in the story. You can choose whichever order you prefer. Go to page 121.**

Robin Hood is made an outlaw.

Robin fights Little John with quarterstaffs.

Maid Marian joins Robin Hood's band.

Robin meets Friar Tuck.

Robin rescues three men from hanging.

Robin wins a silver arrow in a competition arranged by the Sheriff of Nottingham.

Robin takes money from a rich abbot passing through Sherwood forest and gives it to the poor.

Alan-a-Dale is captured by the Sheriff of Nottingham.

Robin meets King Richard, who pardons him and gives him back his lands.

2. Look at the events on page 120. Write your version of the Robin Hood story using the order that you decided on. Remember to include description of the problems faced by the characters and how they resolve them.

_____

_____

_____

_____

_____

_____

_____

_____

_____

_____

_____

_____

Birdwatcher's guide

Read this fact card and notice how the information is organised. The information is divided using subheadings in bold. These help the reader to find the information that they need and to divide the text into groups.

Tawny owl

Appearance
The tawny owl and the barn owl are the most well-known owls in Britain. Their plumage is rich brown, marked with light and dark bars and streaks. The female is larger than the male.

Habitat
Woodland and trees

Nest
Built from decayed wood, pellets and feathers. Built in a hole in a tree or building ruins, or in the old nest of a crow or pigeon or other large bird.

Eggs
3 or 4, white

Food
Rats, mice, small birds, young game, rabbits and insects

Sounds
"Tu-whit", "whit" and the long, wavering, eerie call, "Ho-hoo-hooooo"

Length
38cm

1. Create your own factfile like the one on page 124. Remember to use subheadings, and use the template below to help you.

   You can write a factfile on any topic of your choice. You might want to choose a different animal – it could be another bird, a pet, an African animal or it could be about your favourite author, pop star or film star.

_____

_____ _____

_____ _____

_____ _____

_____ _____

_____ _____

_____ _____

_____ _____

Frogs

1. **Find some information about the life cycle of the frog. Use the information you find out and the words below to write notes under each picture.**

eggs

tadpoles

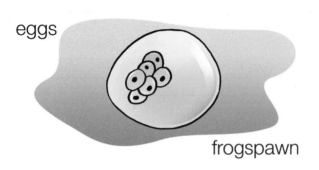

frogspawn

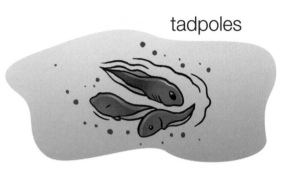

_____

_____

_____

_____

frogs

land   freshwater

legs

_____

_____

_____

_____

water insects

_____

_____

2. Use your notes from page 124 to write an explanation about the lifecycle of a frog. Include a diagram of the cycle. Remember to group the information into paragraphs and include subheadings.

Writing fiction

When writing a story, it is important to think about character, setting and plot (look back at your work on pages 116–121).

1. **Plan a story. Use the ideas below to help you, or create your own. Make notes on a separate piece of paper.**

> time travel   escape   new friends
> the accident   a mysterious disappearance

> at the seaside   in the woods   at the park   at the airport

> old lady   clown   monkey   boy with skateboard   girl in a time machine

Try to group your ideas about what happens to your character as this will help you to write paragraphs.

Your character
What do they look like? What is their personality like? Do they have a family? Where do they live? What are they doing?

Your setting
Where do they live? What does it look like – in the mountains, by the beach, in a city?

Your plot
Beginning – what is your character like, what is the setting?
Middle – what happens to the character, what problem do they face?
End – how is the problem resolved?

Remember to use capital letters and end of sentence punctuation (pages 81–3) and also to use inverted commas to show speech (pages 88–91).

Make your writing more interesting by using conjunctions, such as *while*, *though* and *because* (pages 73–5), prepositions, such as *until*, *by* and *after* (page 76), and adverbs, such as *already*, *afterwards* and *always* (page 77).

2. **Now write your story below.**

Progress chart

Making progress? Tick (✔) the flower boxes as you complete each section of the book.

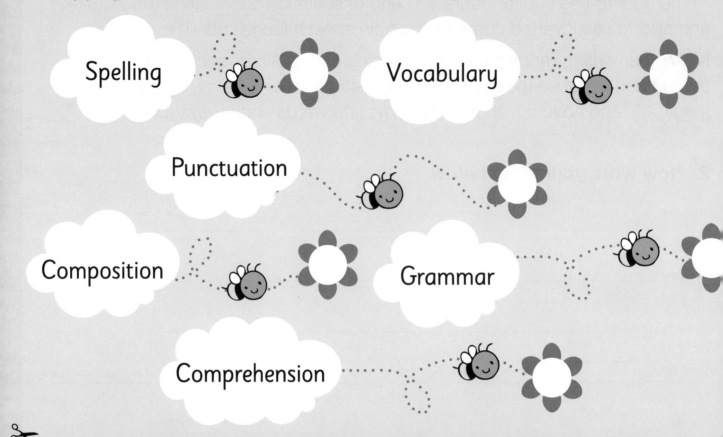

Spelling

Vocabulary

Punctuation

Composition

Grammar

Comprehension

✄

Well done!

YOU DID IT!
★

Name: _____

You have completed
YEAR 3 ENGLISH
Practice Book

Age: _____   **Date:** _____